Renewal:
Hearing God Through the Storm

HEREINZ PUBLISHING

Rein Johnson

Rein Johnson

30 Days of Mind Renewal: Hearing God Through the Storm

Copyright © 2013 by Heireina Patrei Johnson
Publisher: HeReinz Publishing E: Hereinz@me.com
ISBN: 9781726722421

Requests for information should be addressed to:
HeReinz Ministries, LLC
E: Hereinz@me.com

Scripture quotations marked (ESV) are taken from the Holy Bible, English Standard Version, copyright © 2001 by Crossway Bibles, a division of Good News Publishers. Used by permission. All rights reserved.
Scripture quotations marked (KJV) are taken from the King James Version of the Bible.
Scripture quotations marked (NIV) are taken from the New international Version of the Bible.
Scripture quotations marked (NLT) are taken from the Holy Bible, New Living Translation, copyright © 1996, 2004. Used by permission of Tyndale House Publishers Inc. Wheaton Illinois 60189. All rights reserved.
Definitions provided by Free Definitions by Farlex and on line free dictionary.

All rights reserved. No part of this publication may be reproduced, stored in a retrieval system, or transmitted in any form or by any means—electronic, mechanical, photocopy, recording, or any other except brief quotations in printed reviews, without the prior permission of the publisher.
Cover and interior design: By Heireina Johnson for HeReinz Publishing
Printed in the USA

30 Days of Mind Renewal

Dedications

I dedicate this work of Mind Renewal also to my sister Drea Pryor who has been an amazing influence on me while walking the process. Our paths to this peace have been two extraordinarily different paths, but we have arrived at the same destination of healing and hope.

I dedicate this to my children who should hear me say that there is no obstacle that you cannot overcome.

I dedicate this to my entire family as we journey to wholeness together.

I dedicate this to every person on the path to being completely transformed and set free. God is with you every step of the way, and I am humbled that I can be a small part of the process.

Welcome

Beloved, you are special. You are chosen. With that comes a price, but it is a worthy one. Right now you may be grasping at straws in the wind, desperately trying to put the pieces of your life back together, but beloved they are meant to be fragments; fragments of what has been broken to be remade into something that will bring our Father greater glory. Don't resist. Bend to the wind and allow Heaven to speak to you, guide you, and direct you.

Everything broken will be remade. Everything lost will be regained. Everything hurting will be healed. The windows of Heaven will be open unto you and blessings you do not have room enough to receive will be poured out upon you. You will not be left comfortless. You will not fall. You will not fail. The Father says, "Trust me with an unwavering trust, and watch and see if I will not make good on My word. I have need of you. Trust and obey."

Beloved, do not be alarmed by the diverse trials that have come your way. Stand and you will see the salvation of the Lord. You are being prepped, prepared, and purposed for something greater than you can imagine. Let the words on these pages comfort and carry you through. May the voice of God speak directly to you, inspire you, strengthen, and change you. Beloved, you are special. You are chosen. With that comes a price, but it is a worthy one.

Rein Johnson

How to Use this Mind Renewal Guide

Chances are if you are reading this, you are doing so because you are in need of answers. Your mind may be in turmoil as you are walking a fairly new process with God, or you may be reading this solely for the wisdom and the self-check. No matter what the reason, 30 days will be a tremendous blessing to you.

It is my desire that you own and have read the I Am Not Garbage trilogy, which includes the aforementioned along with "Redemption is Real," and the "Promise is Sure." As you have read my testimony that chronicles my tragedies and how God transformed my life and redeemed my soul, I pray that you in some way saw yourself and the places that you desire to transform.

Additionally, the workbook "Healing is a Choice," will walk you through how to process your own stories and command them to be transformed into a testimony. As you are walking that out, this guide will bless you as you walk through the scriptures and apply them to your mind and life and hear what God has to say to you.

You don't need the complete package for this guide to be successful. The key is to understand that every process with God has a purpose, and if God has thrown you into one, He has some great things in store for you. Be determined to obtain them all.

30 Days is about reaching your maximum potential in God, and that begins with a renewed mind. Listen to God as you walk through the scriptures. Let God expound on anything that has not been written here. Sit with God for 30 days in intentional devotion and consecration and journal what He tells you. Utilize the prayer points and consider where they apply. Sit with the reflective questions and answer them honestly. Add your own if you like. The key is to create the experience that works for you. I pray that as you walk through 30 Days you will be abundantly blessed.

You didn't choose me. I chose you. I appointed you to go and produce lasting fruit, so that the Father will give you whatever you ask for, using My name.
-John 15:16

1

    Beloved, I remember fashioning you in the womb. Even then I had a plan in place for your existence. I knew what you would face in life with a bird's eye view from the beginning to the end and the end back to the beginning. I knew then in my infinite wisdom all of the things that you would be a divine answer to in the world.

    I have seen every fragment of your life, every stop post, every place of grief and loss, and for each one I have a plan for your redemption if you will trust Me. It may feel as if I am far away, you may not understand every move of My hand, you may not even be completely comfortable with where you find yourself at this very moment, but I have not forsaken you. In it all I have been steering, redirecting, guiding, and loving you all of the way through.

    Now that I have your attention, I can put my ultimate plan into action. What is that plan you ask? It is to raise you up before nations and prove you as a producing vessel for the Kingdom of Heaven. Your past is not merely your past. It is your redemption and what will be used to redeem so many others. You didn't ask for the journey, but I have chosen you because I trust your heart, mind, body, and soul. I trust you with my people. I trust you with My Words. I trust that your heart will not become prideful and that you will not steal my glory.

    When I give the call for the production of fruit, I must choose those that are capable, pure, and willing to labor before Me. I have been hard pressed to find those vessels, even amongst the most religious, but you, you are different. I can work with a seed. In you there is a seed of willingness, a seed of searching, a seed of hope, and a seed of love and humility. I am reaching deep into you and causing a spiritual harvest to come forth; one that cannot be tainted by false doctrines and religious rituals. What I am producing in you reaches deep into everlasting to everlasting. You will tell many about Me. You will provide the love and compassion that is lacking in the earth. You will extend to others the same truths and loving kindness that I have extended to you, and that pleases Me greatly.

    Don't worry about what it looks like. Do not fear My voice. I am with you always, and I will provide the step-by-step strategy that you need to accomplish My perfect will.

    I am not a God who forgets. Every sacrifice is registered and My right hand is equipped to recompense you beyond your wildest dreams. What I remove I will replace with greater. What I promise I will make provision for. What I speak I will accomplish, and what you desire, what you share with Me from the innermost parts of your being will I hear and perform for the asking. Walk with Me. Talk with Me. Search the things of the deep and see if I won't meet you at every place and answer every question. Turmoil is easy for Me. Provision is easy for Me. Promise is easy for Me. I will honor every sacrifice, every tear, every word, and every prayer in accordance to My will. I want to show you the mysteries and take you to unknown places in Me. Will you come? Will you partake in a process that will change your life? If you answer yes, you will marvel at what shall be performed through you and for you.

    I will teach you how to trust Me. I will increase and expand your faith. I will perform many miracles in your favor. I will show you how to win. All I need from you is a "yes."

Prayer Points:
- ❖ Yielding completely
- ❖ Instruction & Insight
- ❖ Trusting the Process

30 Days of Mind Renewal

Reflective Questions:

1. What is it you believe you are purposed to do? Has God confirmed it?

2. Identify some specific areas where you lack in faith and/or trust and commit to taking those things before the LORD in prayer.

3. What in your life may be currently hindering a complete yes to God?

4. What are your deepest desires? Pray about whether they are placed in your heart above God and ask Him to help you through while you wait.

5. Talk to God about what you fear most about the process, change, and transformation. Be completely honest. He knows it anyway. Give God a chance to answer your questions lest you spend more time in the process than is necessary.

Rein Johnson

Yet He did not waiver through unbelief regarding the promise of God, but was strengthened in his faith and gave glory to God, being fully persuaded that God had power to do what He had promised.
-Romans 4:20-21

2

My child, I desire to bring you to full persuasion of who I am and what I am capable of accomplishing. Believing for the invisible may seem daunting and pointless. You may feel like you are living in the white noise without a clear vision of the future. That is the faith building process. I test you and at times I may even grow silent because I am teaching you even in these things how to stand when you cannot see or hear Me. I am bringing your conviction about me to a sure place, and in order to prove to you who I am, I must take measures that will reach into your heart and show you that I am God. I will have nothing above or before Me. I am a jealous God. If I took it, it was not to punish you but to teach you. My ways and my thoughts are higher than yours. You cannot even imagine in your most radical dreams the depths and the heights I have in store for you. What you want now is based on a limited view. What I want for you is incomprehensible!

So, I begin with a gutting. When I have turned over your life, I sift through it with you, keeping what is relevant, and discarding what is not. I am a loving God, so you won't be comfortless in the process.

Next, I engage in faith work that will push you to some drastic limits, but when you are standing on the other side of the test you will see how strong you are, how vigilant you are, and how powerful you are. I want you to celebrate what you are capable of, and to give Me the glory as the loving Father I am showing you I am.

I want your confidence in Me to be strong. Faith is not based on hoping that I will do what you need. Faith is *knowing* that I will. When you approach a staircase, you never stop to ask each stair if it will hold you up so that you can reach the next floor. You don't beg the stairs to get you to your destination. You run up and down stairs freely because you expect them to be stairs. You just know they will accomplish the job of allowing you to get to and fro. I want that same confidence you have for stairs placed onto Me. I want you to expect me to be God. I own it all. I see it all. I know it all. I hold it all. I created you. Why wouldn't I care for you? Why wouldn't you trust me just because you can't see me? I want you to get to a place in me where there is no doubt about who I am, and that takes faith practice. This is why I test you, not to torture you, but to grow you. When you are "grown" in me; an "adult" in your faith, I can do miraculous things in your life.

Do you fear the time it will take? Why? I have been patiently waiting for you to get out of My way and out of your own way all of your life. I can do in thirty seconds what you have been crying and wrestling over for thirty years. I don't gently peel off the Bandage. I quickly remove them so that the pain is not as intense and prolonged. When you resist Me, even with your words of fear, and anxious behavior, it's a slowly peeled Bandage causing you more pain that I never intended.

When you waiver, I cannot release what is in my hand. You will find that you will spend less time with me in the process of cleansing and resurrection than the many years you will spend in your life missing my purpose and my plan. How much have you already forfeited questioning me? It grieves me when you pass up blessings. I want you to have it all. I want you to be fully persuaded that if I said it, I will accomplish it. You may not understand my path to what your requests are, but if you obey Me, I am sure to get you to your destination. Stand with me and let your faith be strengthened. Walk with me and be fortified. Let me show you step-by-step what your obedience to me is accomplishing. I understand human ailments. I watched my Son bear the ultimate pain. I am not oblivious to how you feel when I remove a relationship or something you have made an idol both knowingly and unknowingly. I see your tears and understand how things hurt your heart when I tell you to quit, walk away, or let it go. If you lean on me, I will comfort you. I will handle it all. I just need you to listen to me and let me soothe your soul. I know what is best for you, and I want you to know that I am good for you. I never fail. I never miss. I never make a mistake. It is always my ultimate plan to walk you right into my glory. Trust me. Don't waiver. Stand even when it hurts and your legs are wobbly. I won't let your life fall on my watch. These are not words. These are promises!

Prayer Points:
- ❖ Fortify Me
- ❖ Show/tell me where I am wavering in my trust
- ❖ Remove my Idols

Reflective Questions:

1. What has God asked you to do that you are wrestling with?

2. What has God told you to do that you have not done yet?

3. Encourage yourself. What ways have you seen God change you, your thinking?

4. What has God done for you recently? Reflect to fortify your faith.

5. Tell God where it hurts the most.

Rein Johnson

Cast all your anxieties on Him because He cares for you.
-1Peter 5:7

3

    Let me first say that I understand anxiety. When I start walking through your life, moving things around, weeding things out of it, changing your course of direction and personal plans, and making demands, it will not feel good to the human heart. Many emotions raise up. Many feelings come to the surface. Because I know the condition of the human heart, I give you time to grieve. I watch over you as you go through all five stages of grief, and when you lean on me I can get you through them gracefully. There is nothing about your heart that I don't understand. You don't have a feeling I didn't create before the beginning of human life and the fall of man. So, you should know that I understand it all. I make allotment for you to cry and scream and question me because I love you.

    There is a point in your grief that I expect you to walk through it with me. To do anything otherwise is to paint me out in your mind to be a distant and heartless God whether you actually say it aloud or not. I ask you to throw everything at me because I want it all. I want it off your mind. I want it off your heart and chest. I want the stress from your shoulders. I want the tears to stop as much as you do. So, throw it all at me. Tell me where it hurts. Tell me that you are mad about what is going on in your life. Tell me you are afraid. Tell me your every feeling and watch and see if I don't show up to soothe you even when I have to correct you.

    I care for you beloved. I do all things for your good. I am a Father and a friend, a healer, and a comforter. I know when you are hurting and paranoid, when you are anxious and feeling deceived. I want us to have good communication between us. So much of what I have to say, if you make the decision to cry to me and not away from Me, will answer your questions and explain away the pain. I will share enough to help you through the turmoil because I love you and care about everything that concerns you. Throw it at Me. I can literally catch it and take it.

Prayer Points:
- ❖ Ease the Pain
- ❖ Walk me through the Plan
- ❖ Help me through my anxiety

Reflective Questions:

1. What are you most anxious about right now as you walk the process with God? Why?

2. What has God revealed to you about yourself and that anxiety? Where is the root of it? Can it be traced back to any childhood issues or trauma or present trauma?

3. Assess your grieving process if you are experiencing any emotional turmoil. Is there a stage that you keep revisiting? Reflect on why. (Stages of grief are in order- denial/isolation, anger, bargaining, depression, and acceptance)

4. What has God revealed to you about His plan for you in the places you are most anxious? Have you embraced it? Are there places you are rejecting it or wrestling with it?

5. What do you feel you need most from God right at this moment specifically to get you through the process? Tell/ask God and let God answer.

If you follow My decrees and are careful to obey My commands, I will send you the seasonal rains. The land will then yield its crops, and the trees of the field will produce their fruit. Your threshing season will overlap with the grape harvest, and your grape harvest will overlap with the season of planting grain. You will eat your fill and live securely in your own land.
-Leviticus 26:3-5

4

    In the garden, I gave Adam and Eve free reign and access to everything in the garden. I wish that you could have seen it in all of its splendor. Trees were luscious and ripe with fruit that never spoiled. There was a plethora of selection to be hunted – the choicest of meat and the purest of the fish in the sea. The rolling hills were breath taking and the mountain views were sweeping and awe inspiring. The grass was a beautiful green soft and lush beneath their feet. The seas glistened and the flowers bloomed and gave off their sweetest fragrances. My children were free. They had it all. It pleased me to allow them to run naked through the fields enjoying the wonders of my hands. I was one with them and they were one with Me, but I am not an imposing God. I wanted them to marvel at my wonders, get in touch with how real I am, and choose Me. I gave them one instruction, "Stay away from that tree."
    The enemy got in Eve, my daughter's head—the slithering snake that he was-- and he convinced her to disobey Me. He told her that I was holding back from her and convinced her that she could become like Me. It pained me as I listened to his evil and manipulative words. I held such hope for her, but she gave in to his deceptive

pressure and shared that disruptive misfortune with my son Adam. Their choice changed my hand. I had to show them sides of the world I never wanted them to see.

When I ask you to obey no other voice but Mine, it is because I want you to live. I only wanted Adam and Eve to live and to always be in harmony with Me. I am so aware of what the roads you will travel will produce. You only have partial view and emotion as a guide when you travel alone and exclude me. I see the dangers ahead and the snakes at every turn waiting to hiss into your ear. I don't mind saving you but I wish you'd let me guide you all the way.

My abundance is not a bribe because I am some sadistic God dangling carrots and waiting to punish you for every mistake you make. Your obedience to me leads you to lands that are abundant spiritually, mentally, physically, and emotionally. I long to steer you because I know what you are destined to become. Most of my children never ask me how they can impact the world or what my ultimate plan for them is. They are content to work day in and day out and struggle through the life they are creating for themselves. The enemy is in their ear keeping them bond to a bland life while my plan is full of color and adventure and is a plan to provision you. I don't want you to miss out on your Eden. I want to bring you into the full Eden experience amidst a dying world all around you. I don't want you to turn to me for the gifts alone. I want you to rest in Me because I am your Father and friend.

My ways may seem tight, but narrow is the gate for those who actually find it. It requires walking in the depths with me, and listening to my voice at every turn. It may mean coming away from some friends, moving out of some comfort zones, leaving some jobs, writing some books, walking blindly, or giving everything up for Me, but my plans to stretch you are to stretch you out into me and allow you to feel the wonders of my presence and to dance in the sun. For your work and sacrifice there is a harvest. My heart is big for you and there is nothing in My will that I will deny you. Come and gain access. Come and sit with me. Listen to my stories and hear the one I have written for your life.

30 Days of Mind Renewal

Let me tell you how good you are despite sermons you hear that are guilt inspiring and death dealing. Let me show you what love really is. Come and drink and be filled—full on Me, of Me, and in Me. Obey.

Prayer Points:
- ❖ I want to Follow Your Instruction
- ❖ Sharpen my Wisdom and Discernment
- ❖ Shift my Perspective to Yours

Reflective Questions:

1. Who are your biggest influencers? Do they lead you toward complete obedience or away from it?

2. Identify places you know you disobeyed God and repent. Whatever comes up in your soul, let it out.

3. On a 1-5 scale, 5 being the highest, rate your level of discernment. Talk to God about how to recognize it and how to apply it.

4. Think of the promises God has made and things already spoken. What are the contradictory thoughts that emerge? Give those to God and apply the Word of truth to them. What scriptures challenge those negative thoughts?

5. Are there places where you are not including God on this journey? Are emotional filters still running that are challenging your peace? Expose them to God.

Rein Johnson

We prove ourselves by our purity, our understanding, our patience, our kindness, by the Holy Spirit within us, and by our sincere love.
-2Corinthians 6:6 NLT

5

If you love Me, prove it. Do away with lip service. Show Me by your sacrifice and obedience where you really stand with Me. When you fall in love with someone, you want them to tell you regularly that they love you, and more so, you want them to show you. You want them to be attentive to your needs and wants. You want them to let you express yourself and to listen to what you have to say. You want them to be faithful and committed to everything concerning you. You want to go on long walks and take you to picnics in the park. You want them to declare openly their love for you so that you never have to hide or feel like they are ashamed of you.

    My people are putting their personal relationships above Me. They have long since stopped seeking Me and spending time with Me on a regular basis. They are not loving on Me like I desire and like they used to when they first found Me. As a result, those that do not know me are left wandering. The witness of my goodness has paled and those that need me most cannot find an example to lead them to Me.

    I don't want you in your own world. I want you attentive to Me. I want you open to Me. Your relationship with Me does not affect only you. It matters to so many others that I have predestined you to reach. It is important that you give Me your attention for all of the lives waiting on your yes. It is a big responsibility, but it is not more than you can bear. Prove yourself to Me. Stand with Me. Raise your voice against sin and hate. Be willing to be an example of my righteousness no matter whom you must confront or whom will disapprove. I will lead you in the ways of holiness, love, and compassion. It's a critical time. I have need of you. I am hard on you by your human standard because I have big plans and high expectations for you. Are you willing to leave it all to follow Me.

Prayer Points
- ❖ I Want to be More loving and Compassionate
- ❖ I Want to be an example that will Lead Others to You
- ❖ I Don't want You to Feel Abandoned By Me

Reflective Questions:

1. What are the things I am passive on in my faith walk and life that I should probably be more attentive to?

2. Can I identify any ways in me that are not pleasing to God

3. If I am someone's only witness, would my life draw them to Christ? At home? At work? With Strangers?

4. Am I a walking demonstration of God's love? What ways can I improve?

5. What Goals will I set for myself to be attentive to God in the way He requires this week?

30 Days of Mind Renewal

Consider it all joy when you encounter various trials, knowing that the testing of your faith produces endurance. And let endurance (patience) have its perfect result, so that you may be perfect and complete, lacking in nothing.
-James 1:2-4

6

There is a saying that thieves only rob loaded vaults. Why would a thief knowingly rob an empty one? The same is true for the adversary. He can see some things and sense what is in you. He knows that when you surrender to Me he must do so also. He knows that if you ever figure out with Me who you really are, he will lose a significant portion of his dominion. He is afraid, and rather than retreat, he will try to weaken you, stress you, distress you, challenge your authority, slander your name, and shut you down in every way possible. He is an evil coward.

Most often I am asked, "God why do you allow this?" Well I would answer a question with a question. "Why can't you remember that you are already victorious?" Why must you relegate yourself to the place of the victim?" "Why are you even arguing with a demon that has already lost the battle?" These demonic forces are already bound because you live under the blood of Christ once you accept Him into your life. They are taunting you from behind bars and threatening "You just wait until I get out of here," but they will never be released from their bonds unless you unlock the cell. When you stand in My authority, they remain subject to you. I see them, and I immediately come to your rescue under my Psalm 91 provision.

When you give the enemy's tactics rise in your life emotionally, it is equivalent to you freeing their bonds and saying, "Have at me." You can look struggle in the face and overcome it all with your worship. It is true that your obedience and your praise confuses the enemy. He wants you to give in to him. He wants your attention like a bad relationship partner. Don't give it to him. Don't expose to him your weaknesses. My strength is made perfect in your weakness, but that strength cannot activate if you are emotionally screaming, "Here is where I am weak!"

Everything that comes your way is an opportunity for My power to be displayed in your life. The accuser is a good actor. He knows just what to touch to set you off, but what if you stopped to realize that he only does it to taunt you and that you could taunt him back by worshipping Me? His issue is not with you. His issue is ultimately with Me for displacing him. He only comes after those I love the most and have invested in. What he fails to realize is that when you begin to see the truth and begin to worship over trials, patience is having its perfect work, you are falling in love and in line with the process, and everything he is trying is only equipping you for war. It won't be long before he stops invading your territory and you are running into his taking out everything you see. You will lack nothing when you complete the process with Me. You will not lack resources, spiritual gifts, authority, provision, or promise. Is there a trial in sight? Throw your hands up and give Me the glory!

Prayer Points:
- ❖ Help me Keep my Focus
- ❖ Show me how I can Defeat the Enemy
- ❖ Fortify Me in My Patience

Reflective Questions:

1. In what ways does the enemy like to torment you the most? Emotionally? Through family? On the Job? Can you identify a specific season during the calendar year that the enemy likes to torment you? If so, ask God to break the curse of that month or time period.

2. Identify your emotional weaknesses and ask God to help you overcome them. Stay with it until it has been tested and you have passed.

3. Make it a point to practice patience this week, the set goals for practicing patience consistently.

4. Are you lacking in your prayer life outside of conflict? Set a time to spend time with God daily. If you find it difficult, start with smaller increments of time and build up as you go along.

5. Read Psalm 91 and make it a point to commit it to memory and apply it where necessary. If you are bold enough, ask God to test it so you can see it at work. Do so only if you are really ready and plan to follow through.

30 Days of Mind Renewal

...Put on a garment of praise for the spirit of heaviness...
Isaiah 61:3

7

Heaviness is a spirit. It begins with a subtle feeling of despair—waking up to it—and one bad feeling leads to a bad day, which leads to a bad week, then month, and even year if we let it carry us along. You have the power to defeat heaviness. You don't have to run with every ill feeling and let it take command over your day. Every spirit only needs access through the pathway you open to it.

No spirit can withstand a real anointing. When you are cloaked in the anointing nothing can penetrate that cloaking because the anointing comes specifically to destroy the yoke. Every fiery dart must fall at your side.

The anointing comes upon you or activates when you lift up your voice in praise. You might find yourself shouting out in thanks, you may fall to your face in worship, you might break into a song or a dance. However your praise is activated, it releases a garment from heaven to rest upon you and gently lift your head when it is down. It lifts your shoulders when they are pressed toward the ground. Your praise signifies your confidence in Me as Redeemer, LORD, and Hope. I will hear you and come to your rescue every time. Apply Me to your heaviness.

Prayer Points:
- ❖ Strengthen Me where I am Weak
- ❖ Let Your Presence Wash Over Me
- ❖ Guide Me in the time of Despair

Reflective Questions:

30 Days of Mind Renewal

1. What are the spiritual things that automatically lift your spirit? It's personal for everyone. Put them in to practice when feeling low.

2. According to Philippians 4:8 we are instructed on what to think on. What are you regularly thinking on?

3. The Word says "Out of the abundance of the heart, the mouth speaks (Luke 6:45)." Our words affect our moods. Give yourself a heart check. What things are heavy on it at this moment? Give it to God and wait for an answer from Him.

4. It's important to have a prayer life, and it is also important to have a praise life. Make some daily time to just give God the glory without asking for anything. If you have a regular prayer life, add some extra time before you launch into prayer to just worship.

5. Break agreement with sprits that are bothering you. Check out your mind and soul. What are you feeling? What was your day like?

Rein Johnson

*The Lord directs our steps, so why try to understand
everything along the way?*
-Proverbs 20:24

8

When you are in your vehicle beloved, you don't spend your time trying to peer around the corner up the road. You are focused on your destination one street, one stoplight, one right or left turn at a time. If you allowed your gaze to shift too far ahead you would miss immediate dangers right in front of you. When following the GPS system, you might have glanced at the overall instructions, but in route you take it turn by turn so that you stay on course.

I give you the bigger picture and then just enough detail to take you one stoplight, one right or left turn at a time. I know what you can handle. I know what is coming around each corner and I am already ahead of you making crooked places straight. If you spend your time trying to make sure that I am on my job, you will injure yourself and miss what is right in front of you.

I want you to trust My instruction and path, and I want you to enjoy the road getting there. I am doing some great things in your life. You are nothing like you were yesterday, but you will miss the celebration if you're always tying to see where the end of the road is. Let me help you. This is a never-ending road until you die. Every promise I make you is not the end of a journey. It is always the beginning of something. That is why I ask you to stay focused and to manage well what I hand to you. You would not be able to handle the details of what I clean out and open up in your favor. Trust My judgment. Most would never tell their boss how to do their job lest they lose their own and their salary in the process. Who are you that you can tell Me how to do Mine? Forfeiture is always available. Trust that I am a good driver and that I am steering you in the right direction. My ways, my thoughts, are higher and infinite. The plans I have for you are great.

Prayer Points:
- ❖ Manage My Fears
- ❖ Fortify my Trust
- ❖ Forgive My Doubt

Reflective Questions:

1. Name the areas where you have a difficult time allowing yourself to trust God. Why do you think that is? Can you identify any roots back to childhood or trauma?

2. What are you most afraid of in letting God have complete control? All of us have something that we have to press through in order to really trust God.

3. What are you most afraid you will have to give up to follow this path? Admit it and ask God to help you release it into His hands.

4. Name a few things you are willing to release control of today. Put it in God's hands and trust Him to guide you and comfort you.

5. What are your prayer requests at the end of this particular process or season? Has God answered any of it? Do you feel anxious about it? Talk to God about it all.

But don't just listen to God's word. You must do what it says. Otherwise you are only fooling yourselves. For if you listen to the word and don't obey, it is like glancing at your face in a mirror. You see yourself, walk away, and forget what you look like. But if you look carefully into the perfect law that sets you free, and if you do what it says and don't forget what you heard, then God will bless you for doing it.
James 1:22-25 NLT

9

    Conditioning begins in the valley, not on the mountaintop. You have to learn to breathe in the valley before you can take on a new altitude. I believe that many of my children want Me to snap my fingers and will them to be obedient or clap my hands and poof, they are in destiny. That might seem logically easiest, but you are not a robot, and I am not the God of imposition. When you choose the path of righteousness, you choose the process of sanctification, which means you must be hearers and doers of my word, and you need time to practice living righteously, mastering every step of the journey. It is not my desire to place you into position and destiny half prepared any more than it is your desire to eat a turkey, chicken, or pot roast half cooked. I know the plans that I have for you, and I must make sure that I prepare you completely because yours and many other lives you will touch depends on it.

    I don't want you to ever forget what you once looked like before I got a hold of you. I want you to have an accurate comparison of yesterday and today that you may see what kind of God I truly am. No good teacher ever allows a student to skip a test based on their claims that they know and understand the material and are ready to move on. In the process, your word is not good enough. You will mostly only being fooling yourself. The process is not for Me any more than the final exams are for the teacher in class. It's all for you to see what you have learned, how you have grown, and how you can apply that to your life.

Don't despise the valley, and don't try to jump the process. Settle in and walk with Me. In the valley I am prepping you for what is ahead. The road to the mountain is where you put it into practice. And the climb is where you fight your way to the top. Your adversary is prepared to put up a good battle. If I planted you in the middle of a world war with no military training, it would be an imminent danger to you. Let me prepare you, because the faith walk is warfare with some great rewards for those who faint not.

Beloved, just rest. Just be. Stop trying to explain away your condition and accept that I am diagnosing and healing you. Enjoy the consecration. There is so much good news here no matter what it looks or feels like.

Prayer Points:
- ❖ Help Me Settle into the Process
- ❖ Help me Come to Terms with the Changes You are Making
- ❖ Help Me Apply the Lessons I am Learning

Reflective Questions:
1. In what ways might you be trying to jump quickly out of the process?

2. Why, what is making you uncomfortable about it?

3. What are you having trouble letting go of in this valley?

4. In what ways have you applied the Word God has given about your situation?

5. Reflect. What lessons have you learned thus far? Celebrate that.

30 Days of Mind Renewal

You have given me your shield of victory. Your right hand supports me; Your help has made me great. You have made a wide path for my feet to keep them from slipping.
Psalm 18: 35-36 NLT

10

I honor your heart and that you do not desire to fail me. It pleases me that you are sincere in wanting to stay in alignment with the divine and perfect will that I have for you. It has been a journey and a difficult road, but you have endured and stood.

Do not fear a backwards walk. You could not turn around now if you tried. Trust me to keep pruning, loving, nudging and correcting. The enemy would have you believe this is all in vain. He would have you believe that the process is not yielding anything and that you have not authentically changed. Remember, he is behind bars running his mouth. *You* are FREE.

I have lifted a standard against him. Everywhere you walk, you are covered by My shield and mighty right hand. This is not as fine of a line as it seems. You need not be intimidated. The path of change feels narrow because your flesh no longer has freedom to defile you, but the path has been made so wide spiritually that your spirit can run and soar.

Beloved, we walk by faith and not by feelings. Don't fear slipping. Don't fear failing lest you speak it up on yourself. I called you victorious when I called you by your name, and I have not changed My mind.

Prayer Points:
- ❖ Help my Unbelief
- ❖ Take away my Fears
- ❖ Comfort Me

30 Days of Mind Renewal

Reflective Questions:

1. In what ways is the enemy trying to make you believe that you are unsuccessful in your transformation?

2. What scriptures counter those lies?

3. In what areas are you most afraid of letting God down? Give God those fears.

4. Have you celebrated your growth? If not, take some time to do so.

5. Ask God for what you need to keep moving forward.

Rein Johnson

Trust in the Lord with all your heart, and do not lean on your own understanding. In all your ways acknowledge Him and He will direct your paths.
Proverbs 3:5-6 ESV

11

Half-hearted does not cut it. You must be all in with your trust in me, or you really don't trust me at all. I can only move based on your faith, a wavering faith wavers and ceases my hand.

Wavering faith comes when you are leaning too much on what your rational mind can understand. The problem with that is I am not a rational God. Everything I do defies logic and rationale. The jobs you have held, the way you got that house or car, the children you birthed, the spouse you married, the ministry you birthed, none of it makes any sense if you look closely enough at yourself and at Me. I don't use a GPS system you would understand. Most of what I do in your favor is "calculatedly random!"

I don't do things the way I do to punish you. I do it the way that I do to keep you safe. The enemy can never know my plans, and because he has studied you, I have to shake you up a bit. I have to change your praise. I have to take you through the stormy route where he cannot totally track your spiritual footprints.

I also don't leave you completely out of the process. You can stand on the sidelines complaining, or you can join me in the walk. The longer I have to wait for you to get it together at every crosswalk is the longer it takes us to get to our destination. The more consistent you are in yielding to Me, the faster you can reach the other side.

Trust that there is an expected end, but understand that is only the beginning of something new. We will always be on a journey together, so settle in and trust Me. Follow Me. If you can't hear my voice, keep doing what I told you to do the last time you heard it. I will speak again. I may just need you to seek me harder.

Prayer Points:
- ❖ Help Me to Keep Moving Forward
- ❖ Don't allow me to get away with Complaining
- ❖ Continue to Direct my Path

Reflective Questions:

1. What does it mean to you to really trust God?

2. Benchmark that definition against the Word. Did it match?

3. Are you living the definition?

4. In what ways do you need to improve in trusting?

5. Can you identify any current hindrances? Give them to God and commit to changing.

30 Days of Mind Renewal

In His kindness, God called you to share in His eternal glory by means of Christ Jesus. So after you have suffered a while, He will restore, support, and strengthen you, and he will place you on a firm foundation.
-1Peter 5:10 NLT

12

First, you must remember that it is in My kindness that I called you. I looked beyond your faults, past, present, and future, and I still called your name. I still chose to include you in the resurrection power long before you were born. I let them crucify my only Son to save you long before you were fashioned in the womb.

The fact is you owe Me. Your cross is nothing like Christ's. Your lashes and stripes pale in comparison. Your grief will never outdo His at Calvary. It is indeed, when you consider the cross, a pleasure to suffer with Me. Your suffering is not Me letting the enemy run rampant in your life. Your suffering stems from what I am removing, what I am cutting out of you, what I am taking you away from, what I am pruning, what I am speaking, and what I am touching. It's a flesh and spiritual struggle that largely stems from what you perceive as all of My "no's." On occasion, you may experience more drastic pain, but even in that I have always been there.

Trust that this affliction is light. I would not allow more than you can bear. I would not harm you in any way, nor would I abandon you. Go through the process of breaking and destroying yokes, breaking soul ties, Breaking chains, renouncing generational curses, and transforming. It is going to cause some personal anguish, but on the other side is freedom and greatness!

Prayer Points:
- ❖ Forgive me For Complaining

- ❖ Help me Honor You in my Suffering
- ❖ Set me Free From Every Lingering Bond of the Past

Reflective Questions:

1. What generational curses can you identify? Sit with God and break them one by one.

2. What soul ties can you identify? Sit with God and break them one by one.

3. Consider your present/recent sufferings. What have you learned? What did you overcome?

4. In what ways will you commit to honoring God in your suffering?

5. In what ways can you identify God's glory in your present/recent sufferings?

Rein Johnson

The instructions of the Lord are perfect, reviving the soul. The decrees of the Lord are trustworthy, making wise the simple. The commandments of the Lord are right, bringing joy to the heart. The commands of the Lord are clear, giving insight for the living. Reverence for the Lord is pure, lasting forever. The laws of the Lord are true, each one is fair.
-Psalm 19: 7-9 NLT

13

  Fall in love with my instruction. Yearn for My wisdom. In it you will find peace of mind and soothing for your soul. What your flesh rejects is food to your spirit body. Embrace these things I say. Hold fast to the Word. Cling to your obedience. I am aware that some things feel like a tightrope walk, but you are never out of balance, and you will never veer left or right as you cling to My precepts.

  Friends may berate you and tell you that you are too deep. I prefer those who swim deep in Me unconcerned about the opinions of others. You are right where I want you, close enough to be transformed and sent, and that is what matters most.

  Don't despise the discipline. Don't despise the laws. Don't despise correction. Don't despise being set apart. Be honored that you have been chosen. Rejoice that your ways are pleasing to Me. Strive to be your best in me and watch and see if my fairness does not include repayment, restoration, and recompense. It all belongs to you, because you belong to Me.

Prayer Points
- Help me Keep My Focus
- Open Up Revelation and Instruction to Me
- Give me Wisdom

Reflective Questions:

1. In what ways can you serve God more?

2. Considering your current place spiritually, what things are you finding difficult about this walk? What are some solutions? What's easiest? Celebrate that.

3. Make a commitment to consecrate over your areas of weakness asking God to strengthen you in those areas. Include fasting if you can.

4. When you consider this text aside from the exhortation, how is it speaking to you?

5. As you consider what the text means to you, what areas in your life do you need to work on in order to honor God through this scripture?

30 Days of Mind Renewal

Make thankfulness your sacrifice to God, and keep the vows you made to the Most High. Then call on Me when you are in trouble, and I will rescue you, and you will give Me glory.
-Psalm 50:14-15 NLT

14

First beloved, be grateful. Most of my children don't understand just how bad things really could be. In certain parts of the world there is privilege (even if limited to some), and in others there are conditions not fit for animals. Your worst day could be somebody's best. There is always someone worse off willing to trade places with you. When you really develop appreciation for what I have already done, I can release into your hands so much more. There is nothing worse than when a parent sacrifices for a child and the child does not say, "Thank you" and belittles the gift. Parents are hard pressed to do anything else for them until that child learns the lesson of gratitude. How much more do you think it hurts Me when I keep extending myself and My precepts are rejected, My words are ignored, and My commandments forgotten. Show Me some gratitude, Honor what you have and the way I am working in your life. Exchange your complaints for thankfulness.

Then you can call on Me and I will rescue you. When your heart is for Me, when you are chasing after me, when you fall in love with correction, when you make suffering your portion, we become one. There can be no separation between us because I will be drawn to your praise and your life pledged to Me. It pleases Me when you glorify Me with your whole life.

30 Days of Mind Renewal

Prayer Points:
- ❖ Forgive my Ungratefulness
- ❖ I Repent for Complaining
- ❖ I Want to Glorify You with My Whole Life

Reflective Questions:

1. What have you been complaining about lately?

2. Make a list of things that you are grateful for.

3. In what ways can you commit to showing God gratitude?

4. What have you forgotten to be grateful for? Go back and give God praise for those things.

5. Ask God if there are ways that you are withholding His hand of blessing.

Rein Johnson

30 Days of Mind Renewal

When the poor and needy search for water and there is none, and their tongues are parched from thirst, then I, the Lord, will answer them. I, the God of Israel, will never abandon them.
-Isaiah 41:17 NLT

15

This journey will lead you into some desolate dry valleys. You will be parched, and there will be many days that you will feel like you can't go on. Your endurance is being fortified. Your faith is being tested. Your strength is on trial, and your heart will be heavy. You will cry out to Me and ask me to stop. You will call unto Me and ask Me when it all will end. You will beg me for breakthrough, and I will not pull you out of the wilderness before your time, but I will send rain to the dessert.

When a mother is teaching her baby to walk, she stands him up and lets him go understanding he may fall, but she is there to watch over him until he takes off on his own. When he approaches stairs she gently teaches him how to crawl his way up and down them watching over him so as not to let him tumble. So too am I doing this for you. I have placed you in new terrain, and I am letting you go and watching you walk. I won't let you fall.

I am there when you call. I am catching every tear. I am carrying you when you can't go on. I am the gentle breeze at night and the soft word in the winds. I will never leave you. I will never forsake you. Call on Me and I will hear. You are not abandoned. Fall into Me and rest a little while.

Prayer Points:
- ❖ Comfort Me
- ❖ Strengthen me in the Wait

- ❖ Water my Dry Places

Reflective Questions:

1. Take note of what you are learning in the Valley. What stands out the most?

2. Talk to God about where you feel desolate and dry.

3. Journal what God has been ministering to you in the valley. What prayers have been answered?

4. What needs have been met?

5. How have you increased spiritually? What gifts have come forth?

30 Days of Mind Renewal

Rein Johnson

Praise the Lord; praise God our savior! For each day he carries us in his arms. Our God is a God who saves! The Sovereign Lord rescues us from death.
-Psalm 68:19-20 NLT

16

    Have you seen a mother cradle her newborn? Have you paid attention to the way she lovingly fingers his tiny hands and toes, the way she whispers sweet songs in his ear and holds him close? You can feel the immense joy radiating from her every pore. She looks upon him pleased and with great joy.

    Beloved that is the way I look upon you. I gaze at you lovingly adoring my creation. I am proud of you, My masterpiece, and I have no regrets creating you.

    When you are hungry, I will feed you. When you are cold, I will warm you. When you are afraid, I will comfort you. When you are anxious, I will calm you. When you are sad, I will give you solace. When you are broken, I will put you back together again. There is never a time that I will not come to your aid. Everyday is a new experience in Me. Bask in it. Rest in it. I am Your shepherd watching over you making sure no harm shall come to you. My watchful eye never sleeps. Close your eyes. Cease your worry. I have you. Rest.

Prayer Points:
- ❖ Calm my Fears
- ❖ Soothe my Aches
- ❖ Help me Manage my Emotions

Reflective Questions:

30 Days of Mind Renewal

1. Identify the ways in which you know God loves on you. Take some time to give Him the praise.

2. Can you identify any places where you feel like you are not a good and worthy creation? What are they?

3. What is a biblical truth/scripture that counters that belief?

4. What are the roots of that negative belief? Childhood trauma? The way you were raised?

5. In your consecration time, ask God to love on you in a tangible way — a way that you can feel and embrace.

Rein Johnson

My heart is confident in You, O God, my heart is confident. No wonder I can sing your praises!
-Psalm 57:7 NLT

17

There is no feeling like the feeling of knowing that no matter what, someone has your back. You can turn around they are there. You can be in trouble and they are there. You can have a need and they are there. If you need to scream or cry, they are there. When you can depend on someone, you can breathe easier, and you can put your complete confidence in them because they have shown you that they will never let you down.

Have in Me that kind of confidence. I am that one that will never let you down. I love it when you can celebrate that I have your back and tell of My goodness. It brings Me great joy to hear you brag on me and see you believe in Me and stand with Me against all odds, even in the roughest of times. I long to hear you sing of my worthiness. It draws me closer to you. I enjoy being present with you in your uprising and your laying down. You evoke Me, and I gladly make My way to be with you. Continue to be confident in Me. Continue to sing My praises. Watch and see what I will unlock in the heavens just for you.

Prayer Points:
- ❖ Draw me Closer
- ❖ Renew my Mind
- ❖ I Praise You for never Letting me Down

Reflective Questions:

1. Have you ever felt like God did not have your back? What was the circumstance?

2. How did God prove to you that He was there, or what made your perception change?

3. Do you feel God calling you to a higher level? In what ways?

4. Are there areas where you need to work on building your confidence in God? What are they? Give them to God and walk through the process.

5. In what ways can and will you be a public demonstration of the goodness of God?

30 Days of Mind Renewal

The water rose over my head and I cried out, "This is the end!" But I called on Your name, LORD, from deep within the pit. You heard me when I cried, "Listen to my pleading! Hear my cry for help!" Yes, You came when I called; You told me, "Do not fear."
-Lamentations 3:54-57 NLT

18

Remember when I first turned your life completely upside down? In this process you were literally clinging to Me and begging me for peace. You were anxious and afraid and holding on to what you wanted. You had so many days where you cried and cried to Me. You could barely breathe. Some days you could barely stand up or keep your footing. Other days you couldn't get out of bed and didn't want to eat or go to work or church. You were existing like a zombie from one emotional fit to the next, but look at you now. Look at how far you have come!

Didn't I keep you? Didn't I show you and prove to you that if you gave it time, the grieving process would end and you would develop more confidence in Me? Even in your present hurting, you are still further along than where you were.

I see you standing. You are studying more and leaning on Me. You are opening up in your understanding and demonstrating that you are determined to stand with Me. I am proud of you.

Prayer Points:
- ❖ Strengthen Me
- ❖ Teach me More
- ❖ Keep me Grounded

30 Days of Mind Renewal

Reflective Questions:

1. Make a list of the ways in which you have grown thus far.

2. What chains were broken off of your life?

3. In what ways has your understanding of God and the process changed?

4. In what ways do you feel more powerful?

5. What are the areas that need to be strengthened?

Rein Johnson

But as for me, I almost lost my footing. My feet were slipping, and I was almost gone. Did I keep my heart pure for nothing? Did I keep myself innocent for no reason? I get nothing but trouble all day long; every morning brings me pain. Then I realized that my heart was bitter, and I was all torn up inside. I was so foolish and ignorant—
I must have seemed like a senseless animal to You. Yet I still belong to You, You hold my right hand. You guide me with Your counsel, leading me to a glorious destiny. Whom have I in Heaven but You? I desire you more than anything on earth. My health may fail, and my spirit may grow weak, but God remains the strength of my heart. He is mine forever.
-Psalm 73:2, 13-14, 21-26 NLT

19

Beloved, I have one word for you: "See?" When I speak change into your life or answer your questions, you may not understand why I take the course that I do. You may be asking Me for one thing, and I may be telling you to do another thing that feels completely unrelated, but even in that I have a plan. My ways and thoughts are higher.

You are going to throw tantrums because of your human condition. I simply allow for it, because I care about your feelings. I see every tear and feel every palpitation of your heart. I know your anxiety well, and I hear you asking me what the point of all this is. I could answer you verbally, and I often do, but there is something about allowing you to *see* what I am doing that fuels your faith. Often the answer comes in hindsight.

When you look back and repent for your doubt, I simply smile. I made accommodations for it long ago. I do not think you are a senseless animal. You are My prized possession. That is why I work so hard to get you to the other side despite all your crying and complaining. I know your heart is pure for Me. I always knew that when you looked back you would be able to see how all the pieces fit together even when they looked like a pile of jagged edges. I knew that you would turn back to Me. You are right. I am leading you to a glorious destiny. I just wanted you to want Me more. You are Mine, and I am yours forever. "See?" You *will* look back and *SEE*.

Prayer Points:
- When my perception is shifting, shift it back
- Forgive my doubt
- Thank You for changing my tantrum into a testimony

Reflective Questions:

1. How has the challenge God has presented you changed your outlook?

2. When you look back, what pieces can you see God putting together that you could not see before?

3. In what ways can you testify now that you could not when God first initiated change?

4. Reflect on what promises God has made good on and praise God for them without asking when He will do the rest of it.

30 Days of Mind Renewal

Seek the Kingdom of God above all else, and live righteously, and He will give you everything you need.
-Matthew 6:33 NLV

20

    I teach My children to be hopeful. I know all of their desires, because it is I who placed them within their heart. The adversary likes to pervert their expectations, but I am always working to keep them pure. The adversary will tell them that I don't care and that their hopes are in vain, and I on the other hand am always working to build their faith.

    Beloved. I know what you want most. I see the secret tears. I hear the prayers, including the silent ones. I see the disappointment in your eyes when you feel things are not moving as quickly as you'd like. I even sense the hurt and longing when I tell you that you must wait or that the answer is no.

    I long to be close to you. I love to commune with you. My greatest desire is to occupy the throne of your heart. I want to share with you the plans I have for you and how I intend to get you there. I want to show you how your dreams are limited and how I can and will expand on them. I want you to taste of my goodness. I want to talk to you about who you really are beyond the day-to-day hustle of life. I cannot bring you to your tableland if I am not first. I cannot talk to you like I desire if your judgment is clouded by wanting things and relationships more than you want Me.

    Yes I am a jealous God, but my asking you to seek first the kingdom is because I am keeping you safe. I see the traps you cannot see. Only I know how the story ends. I will give you everything you need when you realize that I know best what you need.

30 Days of Mind Renewal

Prayer Points:
- ❖ Cure my desperation with the truth
- ❖ Tell me what to pray for
- ❖ Show me where my dreams and desires are limiting me

Reflective Questions:

1. Think about your greatest desire right now. How often are you asking God about it? Process why you keep rehearsing it with God.

2. Can you identify the places of your anxiety or places you have difficulty letting go and trusting it into God's hands? Discuss them with God.

3. What has God ministered to you about your Kingdom purpose? If you can't answer that, make a conscious decision to consecrate about it specifically. Be determined to come out with answers.

4. What does seeking the kingdom first mean to you? How does your definition line up with the Word of God? After your research, has your perception of what it means changed?

5. Often, God exchanges our desires for ourselves to the ones He has for us. In what ways has God shown you the limitations of your dreams or enhanced your view? Has anything completely changed for you? Reflect on that and praise God for speaking clearly.

Rein Johnson

Teach me Your ways O Lord, that I may live according to Your truth! Grant me purity of heart, so that I may honor You. With all my heart I will praise You, O Lord my God. I will give glory to Your name forever, for Your love for me is very great. You have rescued me from the depths of death.
-Psalm 86:11-13 NLT

21

    I desire to pull you in close to show you all of the ways where religion is standing in the way of relationship. It's one thing to know of Me, it's another thing to experience me. That is why I have called you into this process of transformation. I don't want you to have a legalistic view of Me and treat your relationship with Me as one of ritual. I want you to know Me in the depths of who I am. There are many things about religion that I want to undo. I want you to see what the benefits of a real relationship with Me are above tradition.

    When you ask Me to teach you My ways, understand that it comes with removing any and everything that is not like Me. I will sever what has a place in your heart above Me. What you have always believed about Me may be challenged. Yes, beloved, this process with Me will be to your great undoing just to be reestablished and fortified with an unwavering understanding of what I really want My children to know about Me.

    I have rescued you indeed from the depths of hell through My Son, and I am rescuing you from a spiritual death that is grounded in rules and perceptions that I am not in. I am not a mean God who rules by staff just waiting to punish you at every turn. I am a loving God that has great expectations and plans for you that you will discover as you give Me all the glory and sit before Me willing to learn and grow.

Prayer Points:

- ❖ Teach Me Your Ways LORD
- ❖ Teach Me how to Worship You with my Whole Heart
- ❖ Show me the ways in which Religion is Hindering Relationship

Reflective Questions:

1. In what ways is your religion hindering your relationship with God? Sit with God to find out.

2. As you sat with God, what new things about God were revealed to you?

3. What has God taught you about worshipping Him with your whole heart? What does it mean to you?

4. When you think about the notion of "whole heart," what else do you get out of it? For example do you perceive God also to be saying that in order to effectively worship Him your heart needs to be made whole? What else comes to mind?

5. In what ways can you identify how great God's love is for you?

30 Days of Mind Renewal

Rein Johnson

I am not saying this because I am in need, for I have learned to be content whatever the circumstances. I know what it is to be in need, and I know what it is to have plenty. I have learned the secret of being content in any and every situation, whether well fed or hungry, whether living in plenty or in want. I can do all this through him who gives me strength.
-Philippians 4: 11-13 NIV

22

    Beloved, I want you to believe that contentment is not only possible, but it is real. I know that you had and have expectations for your life. I have watched you work and diligently seek Me for My will on many endeavors and in complex situations. You often have an expected outcome, and I have seen the discouragement wash over you when those standards were not met. Sometimes I withhold what I *can* do in order to teach you what *you can* endure. Everything I do is about fortifying your faith, strength, and confidence in Me.

    I want to teach you to have confidence in the fact that no matter what circumstances you find yourself in, I hold all the answers. I want you to know beyond a shadow of a doubt that I am God, and while you may not be able to see how I will accomplish certain things, you will believe in what you know about my Character. I don't make promises I cannot keep.

    If I take it, I replace it with better. If I promise it, you will obtain it by finances or favor. I think of every detail. I cover every crevice and nothing slips through the cracks. I want you to learn to be content, not just in the state you find yourself in with the sole belief that I will come through. I want you to be content in whom I am and to KNOW I will absolutely come through. I want to break the false humility in you that says you are happy when you are not and you are ok when you are not. I want you to deal with Me in the complete truth so that I can soothe your soul and remind you of who I am and what I have planned for you.

When you feel like you cannot bear much more, when you are at your worst extremes, and when all seems lost, I want you to know that I have you covered. I want you to rest in Me. This is why I test you. This is why I throw you into faith building exercises. I want you to get familiar with My character so much that you cease all worry about whatever state you find you are in. Yes you can.

Prayer Points:
- ❖ Strengthen Me as You Test Me
- ❖ When I am Struggling, Point Me Toward the Contentment
- ❖ Remind Me of Your Character

Reflective Questions:

1. Take some time to list out some things you know about God's character. What does the Bible reveal about His nature? For example, is He kind hearted? As you list those things, reflect on how He has been that for you.

2. Where do you have trouble believing you can do something God said or make it through something you are dealing with? Reflect on why you feel that way and process it all with God.

3. In what ways can you learn and practice being more content?

4. What some expectations you had that God didn't fulfill. What did you learn from what He did instead?

5. In what ways is God proving Himself to you right now? If you don't know, ask Him.

Rein Johnson

Not to us, O LORD, not to us, but to Your name goes all the glory for your unfailing love and faithfulness.
-Psalm 115:1 NLT

23

Your language is critical. I often I get requests to answer this prayer or provide that thing, and when I have done so, I hear My children shift from giving Me the glory to "I"—what *they* did and how *they* accomplished that. My glory I will not share with another. I want the credit due Me. I am a Jealous God concerning the worship of My people, but I want those that are lost to turn to Me by the influence of your testimony. If you are never talking about Me, even in your worst times, how will you and others identify Me as the providing source of their most desperate needs?

Even when you are hurting, how much more powerful would it be if others heard you giving Me praise and worship vs. your complaining? What a powerful example you would be if others saw you standing against all odds.

When you spend countless hours magnifying the problem instead of the One who can solve them, you cheapen My glory and you present Me as a weak, uncaring, and thoughtless God who requires your obedience and worship without really caring for and providing for you. Is that really how you see Me? Is that how you really feel? Of course not! Stand with Me and let's shake off every weight. Glorify Me. I deserve it.

Prayer Points:
- ❖ Help me glorify You Even in my Worst crises
- ❖ Show Me Where I am Stealing Your Glory
- ❖ Show Me Where I Need to Change My Words to bring You glory

Reflective Questions:

1. In what ways has God revealed to you that you have taken His glory? What will you do about it?

2. What language do you need to get rid of and replace with something that glorifies God over yourself or the systems of the world?

3. What problems are you magnifying that need to be directed to God?

4. In what ways can you be a better example of God's glory for believers and non-believers?

5. In what ways can you influence others with your testimony? What do you need in order to be able to tell it and tell it effectively?

30 Days of Mind Renewal

Take delight in the Lord, and He will give you your heart's desires.
-Psalm 37:4 NLT

24

  I know that many are confused about what delighting in Me really means, and what I mean when I say that I will give you the desires of your heart. You attend services day in and out, you worship, you pray to Me, you study the Word, and all of those things are great things that I want you to continue doing towards the sharpening of your faith and experience with Me, but delighting in Me is something entirely different.

  You have heard the word "encounter." That's what I want you to have with Me. An encounter with Me is a divine transformative experience that you will never forget. It is where you immerse yourself in Me completely and allow Me to walk with you through the corridors of your life—exposing what needs to be exposed, uprooting what needs to be uprooted, pruning what needs to be pruned, and planting what needs to be planted.

  Most of My children are so caught up in the whirlwind of desire that they are forgetting to delight in Me. They are forgetting to let Me all the way in. When I am allowed complete access, as I am not an imposing God, only then can I share with My children the depths of My desires for them. I know what My children want most in their hearts as they sit before Me and inquire of Me, and I long to answer those requests, but they must be apart of My ultimate plan. It pains Me how many have started the delighting journey with Me and turned back when they realized that sacrifices had to be made. They missed that I had something so much better in store.

Beloved, My ways and thoughts are higher. When I explore your desires with you, I am often exchanging them for something greater. I am the master strategist, and I have a strategy for getting you where I want you to go. When you allow Me the chance to explain in dedicated consecration and focus on Me, I can tell you why certain answers will not be beneficial for you, and how My plan includes so much more.

You will not like everything I have to say. My first purpose is to clean you up and prepare you for what is to come. Seeing the things that need to change are often hard to bear as no one wants to see themselves as the imperfect and even problematic vessels that they are. I don't desire to taunt you. I desire to sustain you. I will never you present you before any promise as incomplete. I want to break your pride and I want to fulfill you in the places you are empty.

You have to be willing to walk this out with Me. You have to be wiling to throw all caution to the wind in trust that I will not let you down. You have to be so *for* Me that no matter what I don't bring back into your life, no matter what I say no to, no matter how bad certain things hurt, you will stand with Me because you know above all things, I am working a greater purpose, and when I begin a work in you, I will complete it if you allow Me.

So delight in Me. Free fall into Me. Devote yourself to Me listening and learning, shedding and worshipping. I am here for you through it all. I will see you through what ails you, and I will celebrate what inspires you. I will literally put what you must desire into your heart. When you fall into Me and I tell you where you are headed, your desires will shift to My will, and you will cease to beg Me for what will never benefit you anyway.

Prayer Points:
- ❖ I Hand You My Anxiety
- ❖ Tell Me What You Desire for Me
- ❖ Explain to Me My Destiny

Reflective Questions:

1. What do you understand better now about delighting in God? How will you apply that understanding?

2. Ask God to give you a life-changing encounter that will reveal not only who He is in ways you have not known, but that will also reveal to you who you are and where you are headed.

3. Ask God to help you put the pieces of your life together in the way that God intends, trading in everything you thought you wanted for His promises.

4. What desires have changed since your prayer time with God and since you have been walking the process with Him thus far?

5. Think about your greatest desires. If you had to give them up to follow God could you? Would you? If you felt any uneasiness or resistance, that may be a sign that something in your heart sits above the place God should only occupy. It may also be a sign of fear. Ask God to speak to those places and shift your perspective to His. Ask God to comfort you through the process of letting go and to help you trust Him as you walk with Him.

30 Days of Mind Renewal

When the watchman sees the enemy coming, he sounds the alarm to warn the people. Then if those who hear the alarm refuse to take action, it is their own fault if they die. They heard the alarm but ignored it, so the responsibility is theirs. If they had listened to the warning, they could have saved their lives.
-Ezekiel 33:3-5 NLT

25

    Do you remember what it felt like to be let down? Do you remember the angst and the anger that you felt when you discovered someone had information that could have changed your course, spared your life, or kept you from a path that would turn out devastating but they held back? Do you remember how it feels in general when you know that someone is hiding from you?

    Why do My children think I am hiding information from them. I may not share everything for the sake of their soul, but when have I ever withheld what was needed? So many decide to take their chances walking a blind path without Me because they feel that at least they are in control, but they cannot see the pitfalls ahead. They cannot see the storm that is brewing. They are falling for reassuring words from man and finding themselves trapped in sinkholes because of it.

    If I am the ultimate Watchman, why would any of My children ever think I would let them fall? Why would they ever think I would let them down? I only reveal so much because I know what you can handle. I am always going before you step by step and clearing out the path. I could leave you and focus on the path alone, but then you would not be comforted or prepared for the next level. Don't resist Me because I take My sweet time. You will find that my soft and solid way spared your life as opposed to the fast and fragile way you wanted Me to go. You don't know what you need, but I do. If I ask you to accept what is difficult, it is only difficult to you in a natural realm where you are more focused on feelings than on faith. I can teach you how to see with spiritual eyes, but you have to be willing to follow Me all of the way.

Prayer Points:
- Show me Where I Am Resisting You
- Take Away my Fears
- Show Me the Places Where I Keep Trying to Forge My Own Path

Reflective Questions:

1. Recall a situation where you were really let down. How did it make you feel? What were your reactions?

2. When you think about the ways you were let down, what would you have changed? What do you feel you needed that might have changed your situation?

3. After being let down, did you change personally in any way? Did you develop trust issues or become more self-protective and angry? How have the changes affected you?

4. In what ways might you be "protecting" yourself from allowing God to have His complete way? For example, do you have a hard time relinquishing control?

5. What do you fear most about what God is or is not doing in your life right now? Where do you have most trouble trusting? Reflect on that with God and release it. Ask Him to give you the strategy for standing with Him in confidence.

Rein Johnson

God is not a man, so He does not lie. He is not human, so He does not change His mind. Has He ever spoken and failed to act? Has He ever promised and not carried it through?
-Numbers 23:19 NLT

26

It amazes Me how uneasy most of My children are when it comes to resting in My promises. This is why I draw My children in closer by way of the process, because I need them to know Me from experience and not from knowledge. When you allow yourself to have experiences with Me, you learn My character. When you learn My character you develop confidence in Me. When you develop confidence in Me, you will not doubt Me. When you are not doubtful of Me, I can release what is in My hand into yours.

I know that in this life there are very few people and things that you can depend on. I know that you have experienced many let downs. Largely that was because you tried to do it your own way or you were subject to those that had control over you. I am not like them. I am the most consistent and trustworthy thing you have going for you.

I don't open My mouth arbitrarily. My words are never wasted. When I speak, I speak the truth, I speak what must be done. When have I ever spoken and what I have said has not come to pass? I am not like the false prophets. I am not like the false friends. I am a sure thing. This is why you must develop constantly in your relationship with Me. In doing so, your ears are always open to Me and you will know My voice. I love you. You may not understand everything I am doing right now, but I am not a liar. You can stake your life on that.

Prayer Points:
- ❖ Help My Unbelief

- ❖ Show Me Where I am Doubting You
- ❖ Strengthen Me Through my Fears

Reflective Questions:

1. In what ways is the enemy trying to prove to you God is a liar?

2. Is there a place that you are frustrated with what has not manifested yet? Talk with God about it and ask God to give you clarity.

3. What do you need God to prove to you? Why do you feel you need that? What will change if He does?

4. Can you tell the difference between when you are walking by faith or by fear (emotions)? What are your signs for recognizing it?

5. Do you find yourself questioning God often? Under what circumstances? Why do you feel you do it? What has God revealed to you about it? Sit with Him and let Him speak to your fears, anxiety, and doubt.

30 Days of Mind Renewal

So that you may not be sluggish, but imitators of those who through faith and patience inherit the promises.
-Hebrews 6:12

27

Do you ever wonder you go through one thing after another? You ever throw your hands up to the sky and ask for a break? You are not alone. Many of My children do so.

I know your adversary well. I know that he is relentless in his pursuit of you because he is at never ending war with Me. He does not let up, and he does not play fair. He seizes opportunities to use whatever he can to delay, deny, and distract you. All he needs is one way in through your heart, your mind, your emotions, and even your words. The moment you let your guard down, he pounces on you like a dog to a bone. He knows he has no authority to destroy you, but if he can manipulate you enough he can use you to destroy yourself and forfeit everything I have in store for you.

The fact is, he is not coming against you. He is coming against Me. And because you are Mine, I stand guard with you. I keep you in a state of "military" training so that you will know how to defeat him. I can't let you get lazy or locked into depression. There are no breaks in warfare. I will never let Him catch you off guard when you are walking with Me. You may feel blindsided by all of My pushing, prodding, and testing, but I would rather you be in a different kind of "concentration camp" with Me than vulnerable to the attempts of the enemy.

I will show you how to make your faith work for you. I will show you what prayers to pray to send him running for his life. I will show you how to defeat him in head to head combat, but you have to stay with

30 Days of Mind Renewal

Me even when you feel like you can't take anymore. Through your faith and patience you will inherit all that belongs to you.

Prayer Points:
- ❖ I want My Inheritance
- ❖ Prepare Me for Combat
- ❖ Protect Me

Reflective Questions:

1. What are the things God has promised you? Cover those things under the blood and ask God to reveal more about His timing so that you will not be confused.

2. In what ways can you identify how God has protected you thus far? Let that spark your worship as you identify those things.

3. What is God revealing to you about warfare and how to combat the enemy? Journal these things and get ready to apply them because they will be tested.

4. Do you have any general fears about warfare? What are they? Where did they stem from? Ask God to answer your questions and help you overcome those fears.

5. How much do you study and apply the Word of God to your life? Make a commitment to study and pray every day at least for an hour and as you do so, identify ways to apply what you are learning without having to walk through tests all of the time.

Rein Johnson

Patient Endurance is what you need now, so that you will continue to do God's will. Then you will receive all that He has promised.
-Hebrews 10:36 NLT

28

 I know that you get tired of hearing about how close you are beloved. I know that you would rather it just be done most times. I understand. I remind you to keep you motivated while the enemy likes to keep you discouraged. Believe it or not, you need the encouragement.
 I will always give you time to put into practice the things that I am teaching you. You need patient endurance for what I am about to release into your hands. I hear you asking Me why this and that and why can't things be done a certain way. It's because you don't know all the details that go into making a promise come to pass. Sometimes the wait is about you and sometimes it is not. It may be about the preparation I am doing on the other side.
 Without intentional focus on doing My will you would never manage the promises the way they should be managed. You need divine instruction and supernatural strength to manage what I release to you because everything was designed to give Me glory.
 Whatever it is you are waiting for, give patience its due process. When it is complete within you, you will lack nothing, and you will understand why you had to walk a certain path. It will all make sense. Hold on. Trust Me. Where you are anxious, I will soothe you. I always send words and signs to help you along the way. Look for my signals when you feel most tired, lost, and defeated. I have you covered.

Prayer Points:
 ❖ I will Not be Defeated in the Wait

Rein Johnson

- ❖ Soothe my Anxiety
- ❖ Give me Supernatural Strength to Endure

Reflective Questions:

1. Where do you need supernatural strength to endure the most? What wait is the hardest for you? Why? Ask God to carry you through.

2. In what ways is your patience most tested aside from your deepest desires? What can you do to change that? What does the Word say about it?

3. Find other scriptures about patience. What does the Word say about patience aside from this text? What new insight have you gained as you studied the subject?

4. Look at the ways you have exhibited patience. What are the examples? What did you do to achieve it? How can you apply those things to your current most anxious places?

5. What are some key lessons you have learned already during the wait? Journal them as you will need them later. What is God saying you have left to learn? Ask Him and journal them along with your progress.

30 Days of Mind Renewal

Rein Johnson

The LORD directs the steps of the Godly. He delights in every detail of their lives. Though they stumble, they will never fall, for the LORD holds them by the hand.
-Psalm 37:23-24 NLT

29

Proverbs 16:9 says that the heart of a man plans his way, but the LORD establishes his steps. In your heart you may have a design for your life and ideas about what you want to see, but it takes a great deal of courage to follow My path in every area concerning you. I want you to lean on Me always and not just when things seem out of your control. You need Me in every decision, even when your heart says this is simple and you can handle it. Those are the times the enemy distorts the path I have illuminated for you.

You will know when a path is from Me because I will hold your hand and speak to you in the process. I will illuminate the pathway and trouble your spirit (give you that discerning feeling in your belly and heart), which is a sign that I am in this. When you pray to Me I will answer. I will speak very clearly about what is to come the closer you draw to Me. The closer you draw to Me, I will teach you how to cover what I promise you. The closer you draw to me is the further the enemy is away from My plans. You might stumble through on occasion trying to decipher what I am saying, but the more you seek Me, I will be sure to keep you out of harm's way, and I will expose to you what the devil does not want you to see. So, stop wandering around in the darkness trying to figure out if I am in it. Where I am there is light and assurance. If you have to question it, I may not be in it. Keep seeking Me for the path and I promise you will find it.

30 Days of Mind Renewal

Prayer Points:
- ❖ Illuminate the Path
- ❖ Answer my Questions
- ❖ Don't Allow me to Walk by my Own Intellect

Reflective Questions:

1. Is there anything that you are confused about at the moment? Ask God to give you clarity.

2. What plans may you be making that don't include God because it seems so easy and like the answers are already there? Stop and include God. See what He has to say.

3. When is the last time you elevated in God? God does not want us living in the same grace year after year. We should be growing in our gifts and relationship with Him. Ask Him if you are ready for elevation and what you must do to attain it.

4. In what ways have you seen God order your steps and you knew it was only God saving you from disaster? How were you able to identify His hand? What did you learn in the process?

5. Are you familiar with the ways God speaks to you or are you missing it? Sometimes God speaks audibly, in nature, through dreams, through the Word, through sermons, and prophetically among other ways. God always speaks to us in a way that we can understand clearly. Ask God to reveal to you the ways He is speaking to you so that you can train your eye and ear toward it.

Rein Johnson

Don't copy the behavior and customs of this world, but let God transform you into a new person by changing the way you think. Then you will learn to know God's will for you, which is good and pleasing and perfect.
-Romans 12:2 NLT

30

Beloved, if in all that we have discussed in this last 30 days you have not been completely transformed it all means very little. The undoing of you is an ongoing process of learning, reflecting, growing, and strengthening so that you may be fortified in your faith and move with Me from one version of glory and faith to the next. There are so many levels I desire you to reach, and there are no limits to how close you draw to Me or to how high you can go in Me.

I know that you have been working diligently to change. I celebrate your tenacity, but I never want you to get too comfortable or to stop processing with Me. Not conforming to "this world" is no only related to the world around you, but it applies to the one you grew up in. What did you learn about life that has kept you guarded, in fear, made you untrusting, and hard? What are the lies you keep rehearsing in your head about who you are not?

I am glad that you have a love for the Word and for the faith traditions that have been set up around you, but I want you to live and to thrive. That is only possible when you draw close to Me and transform with Me. Let me show you all the places that yet need to be healed and uncover and expose what your adversary does not want you to see. Lo, I am with you always, even until the end of the age (earth), and in all that time, I want to see you transform and grow into the world-changer that I created you to be.

Prayer Points:
- ❖ Show me What the Devil Does Not Want Me to See

- ❖ Reveal to me the Places I Still Need to be Healed
- ❖ I Want to be Made Whole

Reflective Questions:

1. Explore your past. What in it has shaped your present negatively? Process those things with God.

2. In your processing, what did God reveal to you about what the devil is hiding from you? Stay with it until you know.

3. What has God revealed to you needs to change within you? What strategy did God give you for how to get to that place of change? This may be a great time to go back through or utilize the workbook "Healing is a Choice."

4. In what ways does God still need to make you whole? Sit with Him and let Him complete the work.

5. In what ways have you already transformed? Celebrate those things and celebrate the way God carried you through. Often the same methods apply no matter how hard the process. Once you have come through, you will always be equipped. In what ways do you already feel equipped? In what areas do you need more strength?

30 Days of Mind Renewal

About the Author

        Heireina Patrei Johnson, affectionately known as "Rein" or "Lady Rein" in art, ministry, and authorship, was born and raised in San Francisco, CA to Elder Huey P Johnson and Evangelist Yuvetta Pryor. Her father, prior to his passing, prophesied over her in the womb indicating that she would be a dynamic and anointed woman of God carrying on his legacy of high profile ministry and profound commitment to the cause of Christ, and that she would be used to bring deliverance and healing to the nations.

        Rein was saved, anointed, and called to preach at the tender age of seven-- a ministry prodigy often astounding those who heard her preach with her keen insight, revelation, and theological reflections on the word. Her ministry was developed in the Church of God in Christ, where she held many positions in ministry respectively, including: youth and young adult leader and minister, praise and worship leader, preacher, children's ministries leader, Sunday school and Bible study teacher, church administrator, drama ministries coordinator, praise dance ministries leader, etc.

        Called to pursue advancement in ministry, Rein was later licensed as a minister in the A.M.E church prior to a call to leaving it to support her pastor in launching a non-denominational ministry geared toward reaching the marginalized and oppressed. It was there that she continued her work in the ministry serving as a clergy member, minister of music, and youth and children's leader while launching out as an independent and highly sought after inspirational artist. Her ministry in the music has enabled her to minister alongside gospel greats and has afforded her numerous accolades throughout the bay area and beyond.

        While Rein grew up fully committed to ministry in every aspect, her young life outside of the church was a devastating one that included early prostitution by her grandmother, molestation, rape, abortion, and later divorce and domestic violence. Her passion increased for the people of God, especially for those with past traumatic and abusive experiences who needed support and ministry to their deeper needs and weren't being ministered to in the church. Fully persuaded that she could be used to minister to the hurting, marginalized, and oppressed, she began to seek God for the role that she could play in encouraging and promoting healing and transformation. In 2010, God ushered her off of a lucrative job as a Human Resources Executive and Chief Administrator and compelled her to chronicle her life's journey toward transformation in her book, "I Am Not Garbage." From there, God has opened numerous doors for her and established several partnerships that allow her to minister the gospel of transformation and the Word in general to multiple youth and women's organizations, social clubs, schools, and churches.

Today, Rein spends her time in servitude to Christ through full time ministry. She is a dynamic praise and worship leader and psalmist, an author, a certified youth, family, and parent coach, and a highly sought after motivational speaker and preacher who is committed to leading others in the direction of wholeness, transformation, and freedom through the work of her organization HeReinz Ministries LLC—an organization founded on the Christian principles of hope and unrelenting trust in God, who by His power and love has the ability to transform us all-- one thought, one memory, one moment, and one day at a time.

Rein reaches many through transparent testimony in combination with Christian theology through speaking engagements, classes, webinars, music, devotionals, books, social and other media as a means of drawing others into their complete wholeness and transformation—teaching principles of living healthy and wholesome lives free from the pain of the past. She is also the proud mother of three beautiful boys, Paris, Pierre, and Caleb-Lyric.

For booking information:
HeReinz Ministries LLC
E: bookprophetessrein@gmail.com

Other releases by Rein Johnson for HeReinz Publishing:

*I Am Not Garbage, My Life's Journey
*Redemption is Real, Part 2 of I Am Not Garbage
*The Promise is Sure, Part 3 of I Am Not Garbage

Rein Johnson

*Healing is a Choice, Companion Workbook
*Process to Promise, A 50-Day Devotional
*iDeclare It! 21 Days of Prophetic Outpour
*iSpeak it Forth! 100 Transformative Affirmations
*Rules of Engagement, A Guide for Singles
*The 3Es of Authentic Worship
*The Gospel of Transformation, A Deeper Look into Romans 12: 2
*EP "Conversation Peace" The Soundtrack to the I Am Not Garbage Trilogy

Made in the USA
San Bernardino, CA
22 October 2018